BUILD A BRAND, CREATE PRODUCTS & EARN PASSIVE INCOME

ROB CUBBON LTD
LONDON SW1

Build a Brand, Create Products & Earn Passive Income
Rob Cubbon
Published by Rob Cubbon Ltd., London. *http://robcubbon.com*
© 2014 Rob Cubbon
No portion of this publication may be reproduced or transmitted in any form or by any means, electronic or mechanical, including, but not limited to, audio recordings, facsimiles, photocopying, or information storage and retrieval systems without explicit written permission from the author or publisher.
ISBN-13: 978-1500531560
ISBN-10: 1500531561

Contents page

Introduction	5
What this book is about	7
Blogging	9
How do you blog	14
Email marketing	24
Platforms	31
Books	35
Audio	42
Video	46
Putting it all together	54

Introduction

In 2006 I was crammed into a London Underground train at Finsbury Park, at 8:30 in the morning. As usual, it was freezing cold outside but boiling hot, stuffy and smelly inside, as I traveled to central London.

Did I like it? No. What else was I to do? I grew up. I went to school. I went to college. My father had a job, my mother had a job and my siblings had jobs.

I had wanted to be successful – it's human nature to aspire for something better. However, being successful meant getting a good job by either working very hard or being very lucky. And, as I'd been relatively unsuccessful at school, it seemed unlikely that a good job was going to come my way.

So I assumed that enjoying work was a privilege exclusive to rock stars, soccer players and clever people – a private club that I didn't feel a part of.

I wasn't very good at work either. I really hated it. I hated the boredom. I hated the drudgery. I hated being told what to do.

So I retired at the age of 22. However, that wasn't the end of my long, dysfunctional relationship with work. I became a freelancer. I hated work so much, that I figured that if I didn't have to work in the same place every day, then I might hate it a little less.

Then there followed a succession of jobs that lasted for a month, a couple of weeks, a few days and even a few hours at a time. I was lucky that London was experiencing an economic boom at the time, and I was easily able to find work as a freelance graphic artworker.

Most people don't know what an artworker is. That's because everyone who is an artworker is too embarrassed to admit it, and will probably tell you that they are a designer. But for the record, an artworker is someone who merely recreates a designer's work with publishing software.

Now we really have to skip 10 years or so because if I continue the story, you'll probably die of boredom – I know I nearly did. I don't, however, want to underplay the uselessness and the lack of direction of my life at that time.

This is the reason I am so evangelical about blogging. If it wasn't for my blog, I wouldn't be writing this today. I would still be getting onto the tube every morning to be told what to do by people much younger than me, working as an artworker and sitting in a cubicle in a mundane London office block.

My blog is at *robcubbon.com* – you should check it out. To this day, I continue to blog and I would like to invite you to follow me on my journey, by signing up for my free newsletter at: *robcubbon.com/free*. You can unsubscribe at any time.

You'll also receive two free e-books, **How to Market Yourself Online** and **Starting An Online Business**, as well as notification of when my free new Kindle titles are available for download. Here's the link again: *robcubbon.com/free*.

What this book is about

Please be aware that this is not a get-rich-quick book. However, if you do what it says, you will make money online. And what's more, in the process of following the procedures and techniques laid out, you will also grow an authoritative personal brand, that will greatly benefit both you and your businesses for years to come.

What follows is a blueprint or formula to online success. This is what I've learned after nearly a decade of living online.

My strategy is about outputting relevant, quality content. When you do this consistently, you build a brand that is known for its authority. Your brand is then followed by an audience. They tell you what they want, you build it and they buy it. And you keep going. It's very simple.

And there's more good news: you won't have to spend any money. But, if you're looking for a quick fix to success, you've found the wrong book and you need to put it down right now.

This book is divided into three sections: blogging, email marketing and long-form or, what I call, 'intimate' content. 'Intimate' content can then be divided into three types: text, audio and video.

And for all these sections and types of content, I'm going to tell you three things: what, why and how.

So, for our first section, blogging: I'm going to tell you what it is, why you should do it and how to blog successfully. And then the same for email marketing and for the three types of 'intimate' content. You're going to get the what, the why and the how of everything.

And then at the end, I'm going to tie it all together and send you on your way with my strategy ingrained in your mind. This will help you to build your brand, create products and earn passive income. Plus you'll be able to keep going.

Why? Because we like it. I enjoy creating content. I like writing, speaking and making movies. It's fun. And I'll show you that you'll enjoy it too. So, let's get going!

Blogging

At first, I had the completely wrong idea of blogging. I thought it was a kind of a diary written by someone who had a more interesting life than me. I certainly never wanted to tell the world what I had for breakfast that day, and I'd definitely never thought that people would want to read my ramblings.

However, a blog is a way for a website to put out content. And that content is date-based, searchable and can be ordered by categories and tags.

There's no need to get hung up on the chronological nature of a blog. Yes, when you arrive on a blog page you see the most recent articles (these are called 'blog posts' or 'posts'). This means that the website is constantly changing – every time you visit it, you see something different.

Nobody actually scrolls through pages and pages of old blog posts. 90% of the time, people will arrive at one of your blog articles on the website via a search engine or a social network. From there they will either leave the site, visit another page or perform an action that you would like – for example, provide their email address in a newsletter subscription form or, even better, buy a product. It's your job to constantly improve your website so that visitors will stay longer and perform these desired actions – subscribing or buying.

Why blog?

Gary Vaynerchuk is an American whose family emigrated from Belarus when he was three years old. He has a very modest background; his father ran a liquor store in New Jersey. Gary turned the liquor store into a multi-million dollar enterprise, with the help of blogging and social media, particularly YouTube. Now he heads a top brand consulting agency.

He says: "If you're not putting out stories, you basically don't exist," and I tend to agree. I have seen the power of publishing stories first-hand, and I'm going to tell you about it.

I believe that most people should blog. If you're starting a business or you have a message to deliver, then you have to tell that story. Blogging is one of the best ways to do this.

Why should you blog? The obvious answer is: to attract traffic to your website, using your blog articles as bait. This is true but it isn't the main reason.

Blogging makes you happier and a better person

You may have experienced positive benefits from writing about a stressful or a traumatic event.

There was a controlled experiment of recently sacked employees. 50% of them were told to write about their thoughts and emotions surrounding their job losses. They were re-employed more quickly than the other 50% who wrote about non-traumatic topics or who didn't write at all.

In the same way, writing about your aspirations will significantly help your motivation. One of the messages from Tony Robbins and other life coaches is to write down your goals.

Also, writing helps you order and compartmentalize your thinking, which leads to an improvement in spoken communication with others. Continuing the writing habit will stop you from being lost for words and reduce that horrible "it's on the tip of my tongue" feeling.

Journaling your life signposts an otherwise featureless landscape. Writing about how you've done, where you are and what you're doing gets rid of a certain amount of anxiety. Detailing your journey will relieve you from relentless mental analysis – like closing unnecessary browser tabs. Writing helps you on the journey.

Practice

Writing is a skill just like anything else. The more you write, the better you get at it. Blogging is absolutely perfect for this. Your first blog posts will hardly get read, so it's almost as if you make your first mistakes in private. Then as the amount – and frequency – of your posts increase, so does your reader base.

A better writer can come up with text to persuade someone to buy something. And this skill will help you enormously in the future when you start selling your own products.

Authority

As a blogger you are a publisher. Everything you write can be read by anyone in the world. You may think that any idiot can start a blog. But most people don't. And, if they do, they rarely stick at it.

Your words are going to be in digital ink. You value your writing enough to put it out there. That's powerful.

Having articles read by others gives you authority. The authority may not be as much as if you were published by a traditional publisher and got on *The New York Times* Best Sellers list – but it is authority nonetheless.

A blog is a sounding board

Regular blogging ensures that you get a feel for what people like to read. By studying your stats, you'll recognize the sorts of posts that get read and commented on.

This is priceless information. You are now discovering your audience. In the past, people would've paid a lot of money for this sort of market research.

I've known people who have built businesses on the back of just one blog post. One day, Douglas Bonneville from *bonfx. com* wrote a post about font combinations. Boom! The next day, Google traffic started to flow in. He moved quickly and created a premium e-book on his site, as well as an iPhone app, both on the subject of font combinations. Both the premium e-book and the app are selling strongly.

Maybe you won't be that lucky. But you will learn what your audience wants and that is pure gold.

SEO (Search Engine Optimization), Social Media, Content Marketing and Brand Building

And lastly, here is the more often cited reason for blogging: Blogging is content marketing.

If you consistently publish useful and relevant information, you will organically attract an audience. True, it was easier 10 years ago than it is today, but it still works. And quite frankly, there isn't anything else you can do to get noticed.

If anyone says "blogging doesn't work", ask what has worked for them in the last two years and, unless they say "thousands upon thousands of dollars in Google and Facebook ads", you won't get an answer.

If you have a blog, you are at least communicating and the record of that communication will live online forever. Your work will be indexed by search engines and shared by communities on social networks, and your message stands a chance of being heard.

And remember, the cost to you is nothing.

How do you blog?

So, we've done the 'what' and the 'why' – now here comes the 'how'. Don't worry, I'm not going to get too technical.

Although it's easy and cheap, this is the moment when most people fall by the wayside. Don't be one of those people!

Domains

You may have a website already or maybe you have several websites, so this may not be relevant for you. But before I talk about blogging, I've got to say little bit about domains.

Wouldn't we all love a fantastic, short dot com domain name that hasn't been registered yet? Well, all is not lost. There are some great sites out there that find available domains for you based on keywords you type in. *LeanDomainSearch.com* is one of the best.

If you are still stuck, don't worry. You can always use your first name and last name and stick a dot com on the end of it. This is what I did. My website is *RobCubbon.com*. The beauty of using your name means you're not restricted to a certain 'genre' of content. You definitely have to stick to a niche though, even if you may like to 'pivot' to new subject matter every so often.

You can register a domain name with GoDaddy, Namecheap or some such service, it doesn't matter which. Don't spend any more than $9/year. You may want to purchase three or five years of domain name registration in one go. It really doesn't matter whether you put keywords, your name or something completely random in your domain. What matters is the constant addition of quality content.

Hosting

In addition to your domain, you will also need hosting. There are many cheap hosts out there. I'll mention a few here but you can find more information on this book's resources page at *RobCubbon.com/kindle4*.

In the US, there's Bluehost and HostGator. I'm always happy to recommend Vidahost in the UK.

There are always exceptions but with hosting, what you get is what you pay for. Usually, the more money you spend, the better the security, support and speed of your website.

WordPress

The best content management system for your website is WordPress. WordPress is a 10-year-old open-source software which has been developed and maintained by thousands of volunteers around the world.

Originally created as a blogging software, it powers 99% of all the blogs out there. In fact, 20% of the world's top 200,000 websites use it. Today, it is the predominant content management system on the web.

I need to make an important distinction here. I am talking about the software that can be downloaded at WordPress.org, not the free WordPress.com blogging site. I'm advising you to have your own self-hosted WordPress.org site.

If you're using WordPress.com, Blogger or any other blogging site at the moment, don't worry – you'll be able to transfer that to a self-hosted WordPress.org site at any time.

Most of the time you'll need to do this: register a domain name, get hosting, point the name servers at the domain name registrar to your host and install WordPress. I have videos to help you along every step of this process. You can find them on this book's resources page at *RobCubbon.com/kindle4*.

Keywords

Keywords are what people type into searches engines when they are trying to find something. We all have keywords that we would like to be found with. When I started, I wanted to be found with 'freelance graphic designer London', because I wanted to get freelance graphic design work and I was based in London. You could also describe these as 'buying keywords' because someone may search for these keywords when looking to purchase a product or service.

So think about what 'buying keywords' people will use to find the goods or services that you aim to sell. To help you, Google's Keyword Planner tool tells you how many times certain keywords are searched per month. It's important to check this.

If no one is searching for your keywords, then you should pick some others. If more than 3,000 are searching for them every month, then you should probably add another word, as there will probably be too much competition for that phrase. For example, 'graphic designer' is searched for 18,000 times a month;

'freelance graphic designer' is searched for 2,400 times a month; 'freelance graphic designer London' is searched for 260 times a month. So 'freelance graphic designer London' is the best one to go for because there is less competition for these keywords, and therefore you stand a better chance of ranking for them in Google.

Where do you put these words? They should be the title of your home page. In WordPress, go to Settings > General, and there you can enter the Site Title.

I recently wrote a blog post about this and one of my readers followed my advice, made his site title "Java Developer Bangalore" and immediately started to get work enquiries.

What should I write about?

I have spoken to a lot of people who either don't want to blog, or who have started a blog and have given up for some reason.

A lot of people think that blogging is not for them or somehow beyond them, but I disagree. I think that most people should be putting out content into the world. And, if you want to make a dent in the universe, this is your chance.

But how?

Write about what you know. You need to provide value to your audience and the only way you can do that is to blog about stuff you know.

When I started blogging, I wrote about creating PDFs. It was hardly the most exciting subject, but it brought in traffic and work. I made money straight away from blogging – after only a few months, I had clients phoning me up.

Be totally honest with your writing. If you write articles about "how to make it in business", and you're not currently making it in business, you will only rehash other advice that's already out there, and you won't come across as genuine.

By all means, write about your aspirations and plans for the future, which may include "making it in business", but make sure that the audience understands exactly where you are on your journey.

You can write about almost anything you want as long as you're honest and it belongs to a definable 'niche'. This is very important as it helps Google and other search engines identify you as an expert within a certain subject area. This area will be the work or business you are involved in or, at least, an area of work or business that you know something about.

Don't worry if you don't like your work at the moment. I hated my job when I started blogging. As I said, I wrote about creating PDFs at first. At least I was writing something that I knew about, even though they weren't the most exciting articles in the world. Then I started writing about Photoshop and Illustrator tricks, which were more interesting.

Later still, I could write about running a design business from home. Now, here's the passion! Creating PDFs may not be my idea of fun, but helping people to leave the rat race and enjoy working for themselves is a real labor of love.

So, if you're just starting out and not sure if you're passionate enough about your subject, then you can *find your passion through blogging*. Write honestly about who you are, what you do and what you want to achieve, and the passion will come.

Don't think you have to pretend, like I did for a short while, that you're cleverer than you are. When I started blogging, I thought I'd have to know more about design than I actually did. This was a big mistake because people will always see through it.

We are all on a journey. None of these journeys move along straight lines. We are all at different stages of our journeys. There are two and a half billion people online, so it's safe to assume that a sizable number of people will be on either the same stage of a journey as you are, or just behind you. These are the people who'll want to consume your content.

So, 'be yourself' and 'be honest' are my first two pieces of blogging advice, and my last one is something that I see everyone get wrong – this is to 'be specific'.

Even when you are being yourself and being honest, you can write blog posts that no one would ever read because they are too general. Have a look at these two potential blog post titles:

1. How to control your fears

2. How I stopped my hands shaking with fear before speaking publically at a wedding

Which one are you more likely to read? The second one is more specific and also hints at a potentially interesting personal story. There's nothing wrong with the first one, but it's not enticing to a reader – unless it was written by someone famous.

But more importantly, the first one will be lost in the search engines; there will be too much competition with the thousands of articles that have already been written about controlling your fears. However, the second one stands a greater chance of being found by people who are searching for how to stop their hands from shaking in certain situations.

Think back to what I was saying about using the Google Keyword Research tool. The keywords that were used the least will have less competition. This also works for blog post titles, as well as site titles.

Over half of Google queries are greater than three words. There may be more competition for single-word and two-word phrases, but there's actually more volume in the more descriptive phrases of three words and more.

And there's more: Traffic coming from the searches for descriptive phrases of three words and more (sometimes called 'The Long Tail') actually converts better. This means that because the search is more specific, the visitor is more likely to be happy with the page they've found and is therefore more likely to subscribe or make a purchase.

15% of searches submitted have never been seen before by Google's search engine. That's 500,000,000 a day.

What does all this mean? It means that you need to *get specific* with your blog post titles. Dive into the details of your niche and split your knowledge up into the smallest pieces possible. Write specific headlines with lots of keywords that your audience will be searching for and be interested in. You will get more traffic from Google, visitors will be more engaged with your writing and, furthermore, they'll be more likely to buy from you.

Get the blogging habit

Blogging is not a quick fix solution. You need to be doing it regularly over a significant period of time before you see results. So you need to develop a habit to do this.

For me, it's quite easy. I make sure I write a blog post every weekend and publish it on Monday afternoon. It's good to publish at the same time or times of the week (like a soap opera), as it helps build a regular audience.

I can't forget about it, because I always have this sense that there's something I have to do during the weekend.

Another excellent way to get into the blogging habit is to show yourself that you're doing the right thing. So, install Google Analytics and in the Google Analytics dashboard, go to Acquisition > Keywords > Organic. This will show you all the Google traffic that's coming in and some of the keywords that people are using to find it. Seeing people coming to your blog as a result of regular posting will make you more likely to continue. And you should continue.

Looking at the keywords is very interesting because it will show you what people typed into Google before they arrived on your site. This can give you ideas for future blog posts. And again, looking at the keywords in Google Analytics is great market research, as you're reading words from the horse's mouth.

Remember, one visitor could be that guy that gives you tens of thousands of dollars' worth of business, or even a person who could be a long-term business partner.

Put content out there, regularly.

Promoting your site and articles

All this doesn't happen in a vacuum. Google would love you to believe that you should only create great content and forget about everything else. Unfortunately, that was never the case in first place and is even less true now. You will have to work on some promotion to make sure that people read your blog posts.

The best way to promote your content is not through social media, not guest blogging, not some clever SEO trick of creating a link network. The best way to promote your blog is through relationships.

Wherever you go, both online and off, always spend time making friends with people who share your interests. You may think that this will happen naturally enough. However, because these relationships in business are so powerful, you can never do too much to engender them.

Online you can do this through blog commenting, guest posting and through social media. Offline, you can do this through Meetup.com.

You should also try to write guest posts on other blogs in your niche; though remember to aim high. Try to get articles published on the best sites possible. Do this by emailing the owners of great sites you read regularly, and ask them if they'd

& Earn Passive Income

like an article written on a particular subject. This may get you a blog post on a big site which means traffic, exposure and a valuable link. And, it will also get you something potentially more valuable: a relationship with a blogger of high authority within your niche.

Nurture these relationships. Feel free to chat with these people on Twitter, Facebook or wherever you see them hanging out – but don't forget email. It's amazing how approachable successful people are online.

On the other hand, don't hassle them either. Don't become an 'ask-hole': someone who asks and asks, but never puts what they're told into practice. If you are genuine in the questions you're asking and conversations you are having, then you will find that people are extremely amenable.

Then months later you'll find that your friends will be promoting your blog posts, linking to you and asking you for podcast interviews. Genuine relationships are far more beneficial to you than Twitter followers, Facebook fans or any SEO trick.

Email marketing

Email marketing is the oldest and most fundamental form of online marketing. It's also the most effective.

The basis of email marketing is to ask for somebody's email address, so that you can send them newsletters or other emails on a regular basis. It doesn't sound very interesting, but it is.

The 'why' of email marketing

Imagine the 2.5 billion people online standing in a row. On the left, you have the people who don't know you. Towards the right you have the ones that like you, then the ones that really like you and then finally, on the extreme right, there are your friends and family – the ones that love you.

If this were the case, then the last group on the right, the ones that like you more than anyone, they're the ones whose email addresses you will have. They are the people who love you the most. This is so important. The Internet is full of people that 'Like' things. They like you or follow you by clicking a button on Facebook or Twitter, but your email subscribers do something much more 'intimate' – they give you their email address.

Back in the days before I had an online business, I used to spend my Friday and Saturday nights in bars and nightclubs, trying to talk to nice-looking ladies. This was a depressingly fruitless activity, by the way.

But I remember how difficult it used to be to get a girl's number. They often used to take my number and promise to call me (and never did), but seldom would I get *their* contact details.

Why am I recalling this sad tale of yesteryear? It's about the difficulty of getting someone's contact details. We hate to give out our details. Why? Because we don't want to be hassled or sold to. This is why email subscribers are so amazing; they love you enough to give you their email address. That's huge!

Not only do these people love you, they are also the exact same demographic as your perfect customers. Heck, most of them *are* your perfect customers. So, your email list is also a market researcher's dream, as their answers to questions like "What are you struggling with?" can give you product ideas.

Not only do these people love you *and* give you product ideas, they also buy your products. Okay, that's obvious. But they buy your products when you ask them to – a few hours after you send an email. This ability to get sales at will is crucial. Whenever I release a new premium product, whether it's on the Amazon platform, the Udemy platform or wherever, these immediate sales cause the platforms' internal systems to sit up and take notice. Your email list can give a product launch the initial push in order to ensure a decent momentum for months and years into the future.

Not only do your email subscribers love you *and* give you product ideas *and* buy your products when you ask them to, they also promote your products. In 2008, Kevin Kelly famously said that you only need 1,000 true fans to successfully market your products. True fans not only buy everything you sell, they also evangelize. They go off around the Internet, spread the love and recommend your products and services. You can even ask them for reviews.

Your email subscribers are pure gold.

Your email list is much more important than your social media following. Even social media gurus, like Amy Porterfield, consider social media's primary aim as this: getting followers off the social media platform, onto your site and signed up to your email list.

The 'how' of email marketing

While it's perfectly possible to start collecting email addresses without a website, I wouldn't advise it. In fact, you can go out there, buy email addresses and spam them. You'll be pleased to hear, I'm not advising that.

You can see email capture forms all over the web; in the sidebar, in the header and, literally, popping up all over the place. That's because they work. Everyone with a website should be collecting email addresses. It's as simple as that. So, how do we do this?

We do this by adhering to the CAN-SPAM Act's recommendations and by using what is referred to as 'permission marketing' tactics. First, we ask the website visitors for their email address. They then get an email to confirm their email address and they are finally subscribed after they click a link in that email. Furthermore, subscribers to the email list can click an unsubscribe link at the bottom of any email, and they will be automatically taken off the list and never mailed to again. So this is a million miles away from spamming.

There are two email marketing companies that I'll recommend – *AWeber* and *MailChimp*. There are loads of others and they all provide similar services. They provide forms for you to capture email addresses on your site, store them (you can download your emails in a CSV anytime) and send your email campaigns to your subscribers.

MailChimp is free until you have more than 2,000 emails. AWeber charges you monthly but they have better delivery rates, allow affiliate links in emails and have sequential auto-responders. I'll explain what that means later.

When you sign up to one of these services, you'll first create an email list. Then you create a form and put it on your website. This is fairly easy to do, with special plug-ins and widgets at your disposal. I have videos on YouTube that can help you with this. You can find them on this book's resources page, at: *robcubbon. com/kindle4*.

Forget traffic, it's all about conversion

This is all well and good. However, you may find that you are not collecting as many email addresses as you would like. This represents a paradigm shift in your online thinking. You have stopped thinking about traffic and started thinking about conversions, and online business is all about conversions.

For example, you may find that a headline change above your email capture form results in more sign-ups. You might want to put an email capture form below every blog post to get more addresses.

But by far the most effective way to increase conversions is to offer some freebie or incentive to join the list. This freebie or incentive (sometimes called a 'lead magnet' or even 'bribe') can be a free e-book, a free MP3 or a free report. You could even just compile a resources list and say "Subscribe to find out my 10 top tools for running an online business".

Once you have your email capture forms and you are successfully collecting email addresses on your site, you should always look to improve conversion.

Mailing your list

On one hand, it's about collecting emails and improving conversions. On the other hand, it's about emailing the list. It's very easy to neglect this at the beginning when you don't have many subscribers. However, it is essential that you start the 'email routine' as soon as you've collected the very first email address. If you leave the email list for more than two or three weeks, it will start to 'go cold'. People will forget who you are and stop opening the emails or, even worse, flag your emails as spam. All the time and money that you spent collecting their email addresses will be for nothing if you don't email them.

So, send an email to your list at least once every fortnight. It won't take too much time or effort to do this. At the very least, you can write a few lines about a new blog post that you have written and include the link – something that provides value.

One technique with email lists is to set up a sequential autoresponder. This is a series of follow-up emails that are sent automatically to the new subscriber, spaced out by a few days. Typically, the first three or four contain great information that is relevant and highly-targeted to your audience. After receiving these useful content emails, the grateful (hopefully) subscriber will then receive an offer to buy a product or service at a reduced rate. This is what Gary Vaynerchuk will refer to as: "jab, jab, jab, right hook" or "give, give, give, ask".

This is only one of many sales techniques that you can employ with an email list. You don't have to have a sequential autoresponder running after sign-up. Not all email marketing companies provide the service; MailChimp doesn't, so I use AWeber because they do.

Email is very personal. This close personal relationship is at the heart of email marketing. People will see your name in their inbox, right next to their close colleagues, friends and family. If they click reply, it shoots an email straight back at you. And, if they do, you should get back to them quickly. It's a conversation.

Plus, to show them that you are on their side, a good question to ask in an email to your list – or maybe the first in the autoresponder sequence – is: "What are you struggling with right now?"

This is the best question ever. It's great customer research. It allows you to find out about your audience and provides you with great blog post and product ideas.

Email your people with quality, valuable information (or, more accurately, links to valuable information and resources). And then once in every three or four emails, you may ask them to make a purchase *at a discount*.

Remember, your email list is comprised of the people who love you above all others online. Wouldn't you give your products and services, at a discounted rate, to the people you love? Indeed, sometimes you give them freebies.

Your relationship with your email list is rather like a love affair.

Platforms

As I was saying earlier, I started out in 2006 when blogging was relatively unheard of. There were plenty of blogs around in those days; however, it was fairly easy to write a load of short blog posts and rank for various keywords.

I worked hard at blogging, guest posting, online relationships, etc., and by 2008 I was successfully ranked on the first page of Google for 'freelance graphic designer London'.

However, you need to do bit more now. It's not enough to have a blog and to constantly post valuable information and resources on it. It's not enough to maintain a presence on all the major social media platforms, like Facebook, Twitter, Google Plus, etc. It's not enough to successfully collect email addresses and to send campaigns. It's not enough to nurture win-win business relationships with others in your niche, who will promote your content both socially and with links.

If you're doing the above, then that's great – I'll take my hat off to you. Unfortunately, there are 400 million blogs out there all competing for attention.

Small business owners and entrepreneurs will always and should always look for new promotional opportunities. And I want to talk about these new opportunities now.

'Intimate' content

Remember why I said that email marketing was so effective? Because of the personal nature of receiving an email addressed to you in your inbox. When you add the fact that it's coming from an authority within a niche, and if you reply to the email you'll get a reply back, it becomes even more personal.

Due to its 'personal' nature, email is therefore more effective than arriving on a web page and reading a blog post for two or three minutes, more effective than a Facebook post or a Tweet, or even a series of social media posts.

This is why I think it's important to put out more 'personal' or, for want of a better word, 'intimate' content. What do I mean by 'intimate' content? Well, I'm not talking about confessing your darkest secrets – although, let me tell you, giving honest details about your own story is almost essential when blogging and building a brand online.

However, by 'intimate' content, I mean: videos, YouTube, webinars, video courses, audio, podcasts, books, Kindles, etc.

What's powerful about this form of 'intimate' content? It takes your audience longer to consume and gets them closer to you.

Take **books**, for example. Books are usually read on comfy chairs or even in bed. They take at least hour to read, so the audience gets a deeper connection with you and your message. On the other hand, blog posts are typically consumed very quickly on a laptop or a phone, either to find some information quickly or to fill up time when you should be doing real work.

Take **audio**. A podcast can last anywhere from 10 minutes to over an hour. That's an extended period of time that the audience has your voice in their earbuds.

Take **video**. A five-minute YouTube video contains your voice and maybe your face. With one or two hour-long video courses or webinars, the audience has even more exposure to your brand, your voice and your face. Compare that with visitors who spend seconds on your blog and leave, never to return.

Hopefully, you are beginning to understand what I mean by 'intimate' content.

Now, a lot of this 'intimate' or 'deep' content can be sold. You can make money from Kindle and self-publishing, and you can make money from video courses.

I love to help people online for free, because other people helped me when I was starting out. But I also love to see that bloggers, entrepreneurs and business people can get paid for their great content.

The important thing about 'intimate' content is to jump in the deep end and create!

Whether you're writing a book, recording audio or shooting a video, 'analysis paralysis' rears its ugly head and, before you know where you are, your head is full of questions like: *But how do I…?*, *What if it…?* and *When is the best time to…?*

When this is the case, just start! You will always have questions.

Digital content can always be improved. Don't let 'analysis paralysis' thwart you from your goal. There are many successful entrepreneurs of recent years that'll back me up here. Reid Hoffman, the founder of LinkedIn, says, "If you are not embarrassed by the first version of your product, you've launched too late." I think this is true of 'intimate' content and info-product creation. And Mark Zuckerberg shared a picture of his desk at Facebook HQ, which showed a laptop next to a big sign with the message: "Stay Focused & Keep Shipping."

The secret to being successful with 'intimate' content is to be consistent. The beauty of product creation is that it gets easier each time. That's why you have to create your first bit of 'intimate' content as soon as possible. Write that book, record that podcast, shoot that movie and create that product. You'll regret not doing it sooner. I did.

So, let's talk more about how to create this content and how to make money with it.

Books: join the self-publishing Kindle revolution

I don't need to tell you that the publishing world has been turned on its head in the last few years. Traditional publishers are going out of business and bookshops have closed down *en masse*. At the same time, more books are being sold and read than ever before.

The difference is Amazon's Kindle (which is an e-reader for digital books; the e-books read on it are also referred to as 'Kindles') and the proliferation of other e-books and e-readers. People are now reading more digital books than physical ones, and this is a trend that will continue.

Anyone that is looking to create a brand and build an audience online should write books. Now, you may think it's a little extreme to ask you to just 'write books'. However, I am talking about a certain type of non-fiction Kindle book that usually costs $2.99 and contains 10,000 to 14,000 words or so. Like this one, in fact.

There's an old adage that "everybody has a book inside them waiting to get out". However, I never thought that about myself. I never saw myself as a writer before I started blogging. When I started blogging, I was writing 200 to 300-word blog articles. Nowadays, I write one blog post every week and it is usually over 1,000 words. I don't *try* to write over 1,000 words, but it usually takes me 1,000 words to say what I want to say. I usually write these blog posts on a Saturday or a Sunday. So now, I find it quite easy to write 1,000 words a day. Therefore, it should be quite possible to write a short Kindle booklet in a fortnight. Which means I could write 24 in a year!

Writing is a muscle that can be developed and will deliver greater productivity through practice.

The same can be said of ideas and thinking. Your creativity will improve through greater practice. It can be very difficult to come up with ideas for blog posts all the time. However, the more you get into the blogging habit, the more original and creative ideas you come up with. This can help you with writing Kindles.

Not only will blogging help you with creativity, it will also help you with subject matter. As I was saying earlier, you will discover which subjects people find the most interesting by observing how well different blog posts fare, through Google Analytics and social sharing.

Indeed, you could base your Kindle books on a series of blog posts if you wanted. You could even just publish a series of blog posts as a Kindle without any editing, but I like to create unique content for Kindle – at least at first – because the exclusivity to Amazon means that I can take advantage of marketing opportunities that come with KDP Select. I'll come back to that later.

The 'how' of Kindle publishing

It is ridiculously easy to publish a book on Amazon and get your book in the biggest bookshop in the world. I don't want to underplay the amount of research and work involved, but essentially all you have to do is to upload a Word document.

Sign up (with your Amazon login) at *kdp.amazon.com,* and you're ready to 'Add new title' to your Bookshelf. I was amazed at how easy the whole process was.

There are several things to consider when you're creating a new Kindle.

Formatting. There are many ways to create Kindle's Mobi format. The most simple, although not necessarily the best, would be to write your book in Microsoft Word. Use Heading 1 for chapter titles and Heading 2 for sub-headings. You can upload the Word document and it will be converted to Mobi. You can check how it looks in the online Kindle viewer.

Subject matter, title and competition. As I said earlier, the successful articles you've written on your blog should point you towards the subject matter you should write about on Kindle. Have a look at the competition in the Kindle store. Are there a lot of books on this subject, which are doing well? It's a good sign if there are a few. Use the book's title to entice the reader, as well as to contain keywords that are searched for often.

A **description** or book blurb. Write a lively description of what your readers can expect from the book and what they will gain by reading it.

You can also add **seven keywords** when you're uploading the book.

You may enter the book into **two categories** on the Kindle store.

You have to produce an attractive, simple **book cover**. This is very important and most people advocate spending money on this.

You have to decide on a **price**. I usually go for $2.99 for a book with 13,000 words, although if you plan to write many books I think having one of them permanently free is a great idea.

You have to decide whether or not you want to enroll on **KDP Select**.

If you decide to enroll your book on KDP Select, this will allow you to engage in a couple of pretty cool marketing ploys.

Firstly, your book can be free for five days out of every 90. During these 'free days', you'll get hundreds – even thousands – of people downloading and reading your book. Hopefully, some of them will leave you favorable reviews. Also, your book is then more likely to appear in the "Customers Who Bought This Item Also Bought" lists, so you'll get a sales boost after your free days.

Secondly, you can put your book on a special Countdown Deal, in which your $2.99 book will be put on sale at a special price of $0.99 for a limited period of time. Customers will see the countdown period ticking down when they arrive on the book's page. This is very effective and always results in more sales.

The downside of being on KDP Select is that the book has to be exclusive to Amazon for a 90-day period.

However, after you've availed yourself of one or both of the KDP Select marketing ploys (the free days and the Countdown Deals), you can take the book off the KDP Select program and put it on as many different platforms as you wish. It will still stay on Amazon.

Amazon, as you may have guessed, has the largest market share, but other e-publishing platforms certainly have millions of buyers. There's Nook, iBooks, Barnes & Noble, Google Play, Kobo and many more.

Book marketing

There are many excellent Facebook groups you can join, where you can liaise with fellow book authors and publishers. You can promote your book during the free days on these groups and you can ask for the all-important five-star reviews.

These groups can be great places to build business relationships as well.

By far, my email list was the best way I found for marketing my e-books. My usual routine for a book launch is to sell the book initially for $0.99 and email my list to tell them that the book was published and available for $0.99. I also mention that it will be available for free in a couple of weeks. A few people will buy it straight away.

The initial sales will look good to Amazon's algorithm. And then a couple of weeks later, I have it for free for a few days, during which time I email my list again to tell them to get it now that it's free.

During the free days, I will promote the book on Facebook groups and other sites that list free books. And then by the end of the free days, I usually find that I have created enough momentum for the book to continue selling organically on Amazon. It might also be a good idea to keep it at $0.99 for a couple of weeks after the free days, before putting it up to $2.99.

Marketing yourself from your books

Self-publishing is not only a great way to make a bit of passive income, it is also a fantastic way to promote yourself and build your brand. You can link to your website and various blog posts from your Kindle books. But there are smarter ways than that.

One of the best things you can do to grow your email list is within the first few pages of your Kindle book. On Amazon, as I'm sure you have noticed, there is a 'Look inside!' button on the cover image of every Kindle which, when clicked, allows you to look at the first 10% of the book. Promote your email list or – more specifically – the incentive (lead magnet/bribe) that you'll give away for joining the email list, within the first 10% of your book. Then you will be able to get sign-ups to your email list from people just browsing your book – not necessarily from those who have bought it.

Kindle books can also be used to promote other products you may have, for example, video courses. At the end of the Kindle book, you can mention a course you have on Udemy, and offer the readers of the book a discount on the course.

Above all, write a good book! If people think that they have learned something or gained something after one or two hours of reading your text, then you will be rewarded with email sign-ups, reviews, book sales, sales of related products and a larger following.

At the time of writing, there are 1,304,075 non-fiction Kindle e-books for sale. That sounds like a lot but, in comparison with 400,000,000 blogs, I think Amazon is an excellent platform to grow your brand.

Audio

My second example of 'intimate' content is audio or, more accurately, podcasting. A podcast is an excellent way to build a brand and an audience.

What is a podcast?

The term podcast is derived from two words: 'iPod' and 'broadcast'. It's a broadcast that you can listen to on your iPod. Nowadays, however, most people will listen on their phones through their earphones, usually as they're travelling somewhere, walking their dog or exercising in a gym.

The format for most podcasts is 30 to 40 minutes of the spoken word. Most broadcasts consist of an interview between two people.

A podcast usually consists of one MP3 file of 10 to 30 MB in size, lasting anywhere from 10 minutes to an hour or more. It will be accessed and downloaded for free at the iTunes Store, on Stitcher radio, on SoundCloud or via a number of other podcast platforms. iTunes is the big boy.

Why should you podcast?

There are one billion people registered on iTunes. Podcasts are the number one product type on iTunes. And the audience for podcasts is growing.

Podcasts are 'intimate' content. People listen to your voice in their head, through their earbuds, for 30 or 40 minutes at a time.

The other important benefit of hosting a podcast is that it makes you an authority by association. The best format for a podcast, in my opinion, is an interview. So identify individuals who are authorities within your niche and ask them to appear on your podcast. Not only does this build relationships with these people, it also increases your authority by virtue of the fact that you are interviewing them.

I listen to many podcasts every week, and I'm never very concerned by the authority of the person hosting the podcast, but I am always interested in the quality of guests on it. And after a while, I associate the quality of the host with the quality of the shows on a podcast. Therefore, you could host a podcast with very little authority in a niche and, as long as you maintain the quality of the guests, you will find this authority 'rubbing off' on you by association.

And you can use the podcast to drive traffic to your website and to increase sign-ups to your email lists. After every podcast, you can promise your audience a free, downloadable PDF of all the resources that had been mentioned in that particular podcast or some other gift. You can then collect email addresses as they access this lead magnet.

How do you podcast?

There are only a few tools that you will need in order to podcast.

Firstly, you will need to get a decent microphone. The cost of a microphone may start at $40 or $50; however, this will make all the difference to the quality of your audio. The last thing you want to do is to use your laptop's inbuilt microphone.

Secondly, in order to record the interviews, if you are on Mac, you should get the Ecamm Call Recorder for Skype and if you're on a Windows PC, you can purchase software called Pamela. These applications record a Skype conversation onto an MP3 file.

And lastly, you'll need some sort of software to mix down the final version of your podcast MP3. Mac users can use GarageBand or both Mac users and Windows PC users may use the free audio mixing software called Audacity.

After you've sorted the recording side out, all you have to do is to set up a podcast feed and submit it to iTunes and other podcasts platforms. The best way to do this is to use a WordPress plug-in called Blubrry PowerPress, which will handle most of the background details for you. There are a lot of great video tutorials on how to start a podcast. Pat Flynn has a series of six videos that last an hour-long and I did one video which lasts 10 minutes. You can watch it here: *www.youtu.be/bfJERgnOxWI*.

Marketing your podcast

Most podcasts are consumed on the iTunes platform; this means you have a few weeks to get on the 'New and Noteworthy' section of iTunes. One of the best ways to do this is to hit the ground running and have at least 10 to 15 episodes prepared for your launch.

When you launch the podcast, you should do everything possible to promote it. However, the name of your podcast, the icon of your podcast and, of course, the quality of your podcast will all affect the download numbers in those critical first few weeks.

Make sure you line up plenty of interviewees and you have plenty of ideas for future podcasts because with podcasts, just like with other digital content, consistency is absolutely key.

Video

My third type of 'intimate' content is video. You can immediately see why video is a more 'intimate' or personal form of content. With video, you see the content creator's face, you hear their voice, you may see their home or workplace and you 'spend more time' with them if you are consuming a large video course, for example.

Why should you use video?

Video is a great way to show how products work. Imagine explaining how software works using text and imagery alone.

With video you can allow the content consumer into your life more 'intimately' than with other media. Your audience will understand you better by listening to your voice and seeing your mannerisms. Plus, you can use screencasting software which will allow the viewer to 'look over your shoulder' when performing a certain task. The potential for teaching is huge.

People can be enormously grateful when you've shown them exactly where to click and how to use different applications, and they will show their gratitude by following you and promoting you to other people. Aside from the ability to show yourself as an expert and an authority, you can also charge quite large amounts for in-depth video courses.

How should you use video?

Many people will find that 'analysis paralysis' rears its ugly head more than ever when starting with video. However, video isn't difficult at all.

Before you start thinking about cameras, I would advise you (as I did in the previous section about audio and podcasting) to invest in a decent microphone.

After that, you could get some screencasting software (ScreenFlow for Mac or Camtasia for Windows PC). These applications record your computer screen, as well as your voice. They also have awesome editing functions and tools to highlight certain areas of the screen, zoom in, zoom out and add graphics such as arrows and text.

I have created 10 video courses and over 20 hours of video. They have been viewed by hundreds of thousands of people. All this video has been made with just ScreenFlow and a Blue Snowflake microphone. That's it, nothing else!

You can also create slides in PowerPoint, for example, and make a movie of yourself talking over the slides. Although if you do this, I would make the slides as interesting as possible and cut to other forms of video, as you should avoid a PowerPoint-only or 'death by PowerPoint' video at all costs.

So far, none of the methods I have explained involve you showing your face on the screen. If you're embarrassed by the thought of that, as I was, then screencasting is a great first step into video.

However, nothing increases the 'intimacy' of video content more than taking the viewer into your home or work place and/or doing a video of you talking to camera.

And doing this isn't very difficult. Again, you should avoid using the built-in camera and microphone of your computer.

There are a number of different camera options. First of all, there are some very cheap high-definition video cameras that shoot HD video, which is perfectly acceptable for YouTube and online learning platforms. You can shoot HD video with an iPhone or most other smartphones. And lastly, if you really wanted to do it professionally, you could spend a lot of money on a DSLR camera.

But there are two more important things to remember when shooting yourself in a video. One is a tripod and the other is lighting. You can get cheap flexible tripods that stand on desks. You can use something called a Gilf to fix a phone to a tripod. You can get away without buying lighting if you shoot the video next to a window with good natural light flooding through it. You can get a reflector from Amazon or eBay for around $20 and put it on the opposite side of the window to balance up the light. Otherwise, you can invest in a softbox light kit for around $30 or $40.

But whether you're filming screencasts or sitting in front of the camera and talking to it, the secret to making great video is practice. As soon as you press record, give it your best shot and *keep going*. Everyone makes bad videos at first, but the ones who succeed with video are the ones who keep going with it.

So, keep at it. And, if you make a mistake or mix up your words – and you will – keep going, start again from the beginning of the sentence and don't stop. You can get rid of your mix-ups, mumbles and 'ums' and 'ahs' during the editing stage.

YouTube

At first, the best place to put your videos is on YouTube. YouTube is the third most popular site on the Internet, so there are a lot of people there and it is a great place to tell your story and deliver your message. As every year passes, more video content is being consumed online.

Employ basic, commonsense SEO on your YouTube video titles, as you do on your blog post titles. In other words, make the titles very specific and put lots of relevant keywords in there. This will increase the likelihood of your videos getting seen.

You can also put these videos on your blog. Write blog posts which can be augmented by your videos; this will help the YouTube and Google search engines to better understand what they're all about. As with blog posts, you may find that some of your videos do better than others. More great market research for you.

What other video channels are there?

There are many other similar sites to YouTube that don't have the same popularity, for example Vimeo, Dailymotion or Metacafe.

However, there are many more interesting platforms where you can sell video tutorials and video courses. At the moment,

I am making over $2,500 a month on Udemy and Skillfeed. Other platforms are springing up all the time and I'm also experimenting with ThinkVidya and Curious.com. There is also the opportunity to sell video courses from your own site.

Online learning platforms

Online learning websites, of which Udemy is the market leader, provide bloggers with a great platform to make money and grow their audience.

Online learning is a $1 billion per annum industry. People would rather spend $50 learning useful career skills online than go to university for a few years, leaving with tens of thousands of dollars in debt and no job.

Bloggers are in a unique position to profit from this amazing new opportunity. As I have said many times before, blogging will show you what the market is looking for. Added to this, bloggers are great explainers and have all the skills necessary to create valuable video courses.

And they can be used again and again on different platforms around the web, as well as on a personal website. None of these online learning platforms insist on any exclusivity.

The minimum length of a free course on Udemy is 30 minutes. I found it very easy to create multiple courses on Udemy, because I was able to repurpose videos that I'd made on YouTube.

Because of the very high traffic on the Udemy platform, as well as the demand for these courses, free courses can fill up with subscribers very quickly. A certain proportion of people who have taken your free course will pay for your better quality premium video content.

After my first year on Udemy, I had over 30,000 followers and over $10,000 profit in my bank account. But it doesn't end there. Udemy is just one of many online learning platforms. I also have all my courses on Skillfeed, which pay me a few hundred dollars every month. And this is totally passive income – I don't have to lift a finger for that to come in.

But it's not just about the money. All the lessons and courses on these online learning platforms are branded with the course creator's logo. At the end of every course, there's a call to action to sign up to a mailing list. So, online learning platforms are a great way to grow an audience and build a brand.

Selling video courses on your own site

As I said earlier, neither YouTube, nor Udemy, nor Skillfeed, nor any other of these online learning platforms insist on exclusivity. So once you've created these videos, you are free to sell them anywhere.

Indeed, my free YouTube videos are also free courses on Udemy, but are earning me money on Skillfeed. 20 to 25% of my premium courses also exist on YouTube.

But, if you have any sort of following, it makes sense to sell the courses on your own site as well.

Many people opt to use some sort of membership plug-in for WordPress. I use WishList Member, but there are other

WordPress plug-ins that you can use. MemberMouse is another option.

Additionally, you need to sort out a payment gateway (I use PayPal) and video hosting (I use Vimeo, but Wistia is another option). I also use Sensei, a plug-in from WooThemes, to handle the course and lesson structure – but that's not a 'must-have'.

As you might imagine, getting all these plug-ins and online services to play nicely together can be a headache. However, once you have it up and running, it's passive income all the way!

If all this sounds like too much hassle for you, you can use Fedora, which is very popular with Udemy instructors right now. Fedora works on your site but handles hosting, bandwidth and payment processing for a monthly fee. It has an added advantage of offering a direct upload from Udemy or Dropbox. Another outfit that can build a school on your site is Thinkific.com.

More details and options for selling video courses on your own site can be found on this book's resources page, at: *robcubbon.com/kindle4.*

Google Hangouts on Air and Webinars

Another example of long-form video content that deepens the relationship with your audience is the webinar.

A webinar is a live videocast where you can talk over slides, talk to the camera or demonstrate software. The audience can ask questions using text chat during the presentation. Ideally, there should be a hundred or more people attending the webinar. They are usually invited through an email campaign or Facebook ads.

Webinars are usually free but, after an hour of great content, there is an offer of an info-product at the end.

Webinars can be hosted live on platforms such as GoToWebinar, and the recordings can be saved, viewed and sold afterwards. If you're interested in holding a webinar, you may like to cut your teeth by hosting a Google Hangout first.

Google Hangouts on Air are video conferences for up to 10 people. They can share their screens and other people can watch. These videos can also be saved and later viewed on YouTube.

Putting it all together

So let's recap on what I've been saying here. Firstly, I was extolling the virtues of blogging. It's necessary for anyone in this day and age to have their own website. And, if a website is going to be relevant, recognized by search engines and shared on social platforms, then that website needs to be regularly updated. So your website should have quality, relevant content constantly added.

Secondly, I told you about the importance of the email list. I said that every website and every business needs to collect email addresses and should be constantly working to improve conversions (the number of email addresses captured) on their website. The people on these email lists should be emailed at least once a fortnight with useful information. One email in every four can be a sales email.

And thirdly, I discussed platforms and the various forms of personal or 'intimate' content with which you can build your brand, sell products and earn passive income. These were split into three broad groupings: text (books), audio (podcasts) and video (YouTube, online courses, webinars).

Branching out and creating long-form content will place you apart from everyone else online. Make no mistake, the majority of people will not do this. People want instant results from minimum effort. And you will *not* gain instant riches from doing this.

But as I've said already, it's not difficult to write a 10,000 word Kindle book, it's not difficult to make a 40-minute podcast and it's not difficult to create an hour-long video course. Most people won't do these things and hardly anyone will do them consistently. The ones who do will be successful.

Keeping it going and be consistent

I'm not suggesting that anyone instantly starts blogging, podcasting, writing books and creating video. That would be too much.

If you're already blogging, then I would suggest you should start on one of the three forms of 'intimate' content right now, and stick at it – that's assuming you're already building an email list and emailing them regularly.

If it's Kindle, then try to write 750 words per day. If it's a podcast, then write a list of at least 20 people within a niche that you like to interview. If it's video, then try to put a few minutes' worth of video out on YouTube every week.

A journey of a thousand miles starts with a single step.

What's important is that you keep going. Keep blogging. Keep adding to your email list. And keep on creating your particular form of 'intimate' content, whether it's books, podcasts or videos.

Remember, you will only improve at content creation. You will not only become a better writer, podcaster and videographer with time, but your productivity will also improve.

So later, you may like to add a second form of 'intimate' content to your first. However, regularly outputting all three forms of 'intimate' content may be too much for a single human being.

At the moment, I'm concentrating on Kindles and video courses. I'm usually either writing a book or creating a video course. I wouldn't want to do the two things at the same time, along with blogging and running my design business.

Consistency is most important in podcasting. Once you commit to a podcast, see it through for at least two years and post a show at least once a fortnight.

With book writing and video making, it's important to keep going. Rinse and repeat, as they say. Consistency isn't as important for video and Kindle books; however, don't leave your YouTube channel alone for more than a month.

You have to practice your art. The beauty of this formula is that you become a better artist as you go on. Don't do what everyone else does – publish on Kindle once, write a few blog posts, record a few podcasts or create one premium Udemy course and then moan that no one cares about you. You're damn right no one cares about you! There's just too much noise out there. You've got to persevere on all these channels in order to see any results. And, you will see results and you will be successful if you keep at it. *You* can do it.

One of your courses may start selling well, one of your podcast guests may become an amazing mentor and one of your Kindle books could really take off. You only have to be successful once. The trick is to increase the likelihood of that happening.

Filling up your email list and cross-selling

The blog, the podcast, the video, the books and the email list – they're all linked. You should constantly be increasing the numbers on your email list, and all these platforms and channels are excellent ways to increase your following and collect emails.

Create an easy to remember URL for your email collection page where you promote your offer. Mine is *RobCubbon.com/ free*. It redirects to a longer URL. Imagine that you're listening to a podcast while running on a treadmill in a gym. I can tell you to sign up at 'Rob Cubbon dot com slash free' and, if you know the correct spelling of my name, you'll be able to sign up to my email list when you get home.

You can purchase a whole new domain for this purpose. For example, I have *FreeFromRob.com*.

You can also promote to your list through your YouTube videos and in your courses.

Kindle is also a great source of email addresses. Add a call to action within the first 10% of your book and it can be accessed on the Amazon site via the 'Look inside!' button on the cover image. This means that you can receive email subscribers from people who are interested in your book, as well as from people who've bought the book. This is a great way to get email addresses. If people don't want to buy from you this time, they may buy from you later.

On your videos, you can add links to a sign-up page, using YouTube's annotations. And from your video courses on Udemy and other platforms, you can direct people towards your email offer.

But it doesn't end there. You can sell your video courses on Kindle, mention your Kindles on your podcast and create an Udemy course based on your podcast. People who have bought from you once are extremely likely to buy from you again. Cross-sell every product on every platform.

When you are blogging and selling digital products on multiple platforms, the system will start feeding itself. That's the beauty of this model.

Enjoy what you do

As I've explained, constantly putting out stories on your blog and creating digital products isn't difficult. But there's one more element that we have to take into consideration:

Have fun! Don't forget to enjoy yourself. Enjoy creating these digital products. If they are born of enthusiasm and happiness, then they'll be consumed in the same way.

If you create products just to make money, they won't be as successful as the products that you create because you *want* to.

& Earn Passive Income

Peace!

Printed in Great Britain
by Amazon